The Pa   ek

                                                                          es

Amber Verbeek

The Path to Success for Digital Casual Games

A case study research into Angry Birds, Candy Crush and Flappy Bird

LAP LAMBERT Academic Publishing

Imprint

Any brand names and product names mentioned in this book are subject to trademark, brand or patent protection and are trademarks or registered trademarks of their respective holders. The use of brand names, product names, common names, trade names, product descriptions etc. even without a particular marking in this work is in no way to be construed to mean that such names may be regarded as unrestricted in respect of trademark and brand protection legislation and could thus be used by anyone.

Cover image: www.ingimage.com

Publisher:
LAP LAMBERT Academic Publishing
is a trademark of
International Book Market Service Ltd., member of OmniScriptum Publishing Group
17 Meldrum Street, Beau Bassin 71504, Mauritius

Printed at: see last page
ISBN: 978-3-659-83431-8

"The path to success for digital casual games"

A case study research into Angry Birds, Candy Crush and Flappy Bird

Student Name: Amber Verbeek
Student Number: 353849

Supervisor: Dr. Jason Pridmore

International Bachelor in Communication and Media
Erasmus School of History, Culture and Communication
Erasmus University Rotterdam

Bachelor's Thesis
June 2014

Abstract

The purpose of this study is to investigate the process of success for the development of digital casual games and the implications of their success. Specifically, the study concentrates on the digital casual games Angry Birds, Candy Crush Saga and Flappy Bird by drawing on the product life cycle theory. These cases were chosen because of their different backgrounds and as they are seen as exemplary forms of casual game success. In addition, the relationship between social media and these games is examined. Very little research has been conducted on digital casual games and marketing. Therefore, this study offers new insight into the process of certain digital casual games that became successful. Case study research is conducted by selecting articles and blogs per case. The findings show that the process of success and its implications differ per case. For Angry Birds, the process was highlighted by the make-or-break business plan, their focus group research, the design and their plan to rank as No 1 in Apple's App Store. An implication emerged with the statement of Angry Birds' creator Rovio who wants to become a world brand with all the merchandise they have produced, such as soft toys. For Candy Crush Saga, the success process was highlighted by the Saga games, Facebook, the trademarks, in-app purchases and the design. The implications for the success of this game have enabled King, the owner of the game, to start broadcasting TV ads to capitalize on their success. Next to this, King aims to produce a series of Saga games. For Flappy Bird, the process of success was highlighted by the simplicity of the game, threats via Twitter, pulling the game from stores and the fight to get the game back. The implications of its success hold that Dong Nguyen now has a lot of fans but he does not want to bring the game back yet. However, he is working on a different and better version of the game. In all these cases, success is referred to in numbers, such as revenue, number of downloads, ranking and number of users. Finally, the product life cycle theory is used to identify the stages for each case. The results show that the four stages of his theory – introduction, growth, maturity, decline - do not have the same duration. Therefore, the theory cannot be used to anticipate stages or actions as the boundaries of the stages are cannot be identified in advance.

Keywords: Digital casual games, success, angry birds, candy crush saga, flappy bird

Table of Contents

Chapter 1: Introduction

Humans have always played games. For example, dice are older than recorded history (Anderson, 2012). People used to sit down and actually play a game but since the rise of smartphones, the video-game industry has changed. We now live in a world with digital casual games. These games are relatively easy to develop and to distribute through various app stores, which is one the reasons for the change in game design. Digital casual games are designed to be played when people have time to kill, thus while waiting for the bus or during a coffee-break. Users can play these games easily by sliding and tapping the smartphone's screen.

The majority of currently active social media users has heard of the games Angry Birds, Candy Crush Saga and Flappy Bird. Around 15 million people play Candy Crush Saga on Facebook every day (The Economist, 2013), Angry Birds is still one of the most downloaded apps and Flappy Bird pulled the plug recently due to various reasons, among which that Dong Nguyen could not take being so successful. How did these games become such a success? What makes the games so special?

This research will focus on digital casual games that have become extremely popular in the past few years. It is not always clear why digital casual games become so successful due to a lack of transparency of the developers, a lack of knowledge regarding consumer behavior and various interpretations of the concepts 'digital casual games' and 'success'. Moreover, if people knew exactly how digital casual games become popular, they would become very rich by developing a game themselves. Instead of looking into why these digital casual games became successful, this research will concentrate on their process for 'success' in the development of these digital casual games and the implications of this 'success'. In order to research this, a research question and various sub questions are formulated:

RQ: What is the process of 'success' for the development of digital casual games and what were the implications of this 'success'?

4

SQ1: What were the factors that contributed to the success of Angry Birds, Candy Crush Saga and Flappy Bird?

SQ2: What is the relationship between social media and Angry Birds, Candy Crush Saga and Flappy Bird?

SQ3: What were the implications of success for Angry Birds, Candy Crush Saga and Flappy Bird?

The research question and sub questions all address certain terms that are important to elaborate on. These terms will be explained throughout this research. Specifically, the terms digital casual games, success and social media will be focused on. Since this research concentrates on Angry Birds, Candy Crush Saga and Flappy Bird and their process of success and its implication, case study research is conducted for each case. The games will be analyzed from a perspective that focuses on the business-side; the product life cycle theory. Therefore this research will not focus on why people want to play these games, but on what the developers' strategy was and how they dealt with their success.

The results of this study will give more insight into the processes of certain digital casual games that became successful. This information is relevant for companies or developers that might want to replicate their strategies or decide to deviate from them instead, depending on how the game is developed. In addition, it is important for people to care about this topic since the influence of these developers' increases. Small companies or even individual designers can turn into media companies. The production does not stop at one digital casual game, but it goes further into either a series of these or even merchandise and movies.

Chapter 2: Theory

According to Russoniello, O'Brien and Parks (2009) there are more than 200 million casual game players in the whole world. These casual game players usually utilize consoles, PC's and handheld devices such as smartphones and tablets. Smartphones and tablets have become more advanced over the years because of chips developed by Intel and Hitachi that provide these devices with ever-greater computing power, storage capacity and graphic and audio capabilities (Soh & Tan, 2008). This technology allowed for more players and a better gameplay. In addition, digital casual games are frequently connected with social networks, such as Twitter and Facebook. This aspect intensifies the popularity of digital casual games, as people indicate to others that they are playing this game and are incentivized to ask for 'help'.

It is remarkable that not much research has been done on marketing and digital casual games. However, since digital casual games have become a booming business it is interesting to look deeper into digital casual games themselves and their path to 'success'.

2.1 Digital casual games

There still is a lot of discussion about the definition of digital casual games, since there are many different interpretations of the term. Cheng (2011) defined digital casual games as "quick to access, easy to learn and requires no previous special video game skills, expertise of regular time commitment to play". This definition is shared with other authors, such as Di Loreto & Gouaich (2010, p. 2) who stated that "digital casual games involve less complicated game controls and less complexity in terms of gameplay than other online games." These authors also argued that digital casual games are produced for the mass consumer – those who would not view themselves as gamer. In addition, the Casual Games Assocation (N.D.) stated on their website that these games are "developed for the general public and families."

Next to the definition of the casual gaming, there is also a lot of discussion about the term *casual*. In Kuittinen et. al.'s study (2007), the authors analyzed various views of game professionals, game journalists, gamers, reported surveys and more to assess the term *casual*. The data showed that casual gamers refer mostly to consumers that can "pick up and play casual games easily without any great effort" (p. 106). They are seen as the opposite of hardcore gamers, therefore casual gamers only play non-hardcore games (Kuittinen, Kultima, Niemela, & Paavilainen, 2007). Hardcore games are seen as challenging and require experience to play. In addition, hardcore gamers usually play on a high difficulty level and have a large interest in gaming as a hobby (Kuittinen et al., 2007). However, there are some issues with this restrictive boundary as there are consumers that play both types of games, which not immediately makes them a casual gamer or hardcore gamer. People that play both types of games can be referred to as 'core gamers' according to Kuittinen et al. (2007). These groups should not be seen as exclusive definitions, but as examples of how the game industry segments their customers. The term *casual* is best defined by the easiness of the game experience, according to Kuittinen et al. (2007). Kim (2013) disagrees and claims that the term is defined by looking at different ages. Complex mobile games are played by younger people. In contrast, older people prefer casual games to pass time.

For this research, digital casual games are defined as quick to access, easy to learn and that no game experience is required. This research takes a different perspective on the term *casual* than Kuittinen et al. (2007) and Kim (2013), since digital casual games are also often defined by situations in which these games can be played. Users are able to play a digital casual game anywhere and anytime. Di Loreto and Gouaich (2010) build upon this idea by stating that the motivation to play these games is caused by the psychological needs of the user. This means that users are triggered by their own needs, goals and possible incentives of the game. There are a number of these games, but for this research I will focus on three of the most popular ones: Angry Birds, Candy Crush Saga and Flappy Bird.

2.2 'Success' and social media

Research concerning gaming often refers to 'success' in numbers, such as revenue or the number of downloads/users. It is remarkable that these studies never referred to 'success' as something else. Since the gaming industry makes commercial products, it is assumed by most authors that 'success' here means money (Shelley, 2001). However, 'success' can be seen to have different meanings and different levels, such as the attainment of fame and/or social status. Flappy Bird is an interesting case when assessing the term success as the developer's experience differs from the other cases in a way that the success of Flappy Bird was not what the developer expected. The success of Flappy Bird just became too much, which resulted in the removal of the game from the App Store and Google Play. Even though success can be interpreted in various ways, this research will first investigate success as a reference to revenue, ranking and the number of downloads/users. The second part with regard to the term will focus on a much broader view which will be demonstrated later.

With the increasing popularity of social networks, such as Facebook and Twitter, some casual games evolved into social games (Cheng, 2011). This means that either: 1) digital casual games added social network integration; or 2) social networks added digital casual game support. An example of the second situation is the game Candy Crush Saga, which casual game players are able to find on Facebook. Even though other social media such as MySpace contributed to the growth of casual game players, Facebook is the social network where a casual game application has the highest impact (Di Loreto & Gouaich, 2010). The reason why digital casual games become a trend on social networks is unclear (Asur, Huberman, Szabo, & Wang, 2011). However, the most important factors to cause a trend are retweets on Twitter and shares on Facebook which is what happens with digital casual games. People tell others that they are playing this game, whereafter friends will comment on this post and share it. Eventually this results in an increase in popularity of the digital casual game. In addition, players are able to share their high scores and send extra lives to use in the game. The more friends play the game, the more extra lives the users receive (Bell, et al., 2006). These games can also cause new friendships or collaborations when a user plays with strangers. Social media are being integrated into the games more often which almost results in gamifying social relationships.

Social media has not only had an impact on casual gaming, but casual gaming also had an impact on social media. This is what will be investigated in this research as well: the relationship between social media and casual gaming. Social media, within this research, will be limited to Twitter and Facebook, since those are the platforms where Angry Birds, Candy Crush Saga and Flappy Bird became most popular.

2.3 Literature review

Casual games are also referred to as 'coffee-break' or 'web games' (Russoniello, O'Brien, & Parks, 2009). This sector has been growing fast in the last few years and industry experts have estimated that within one year "the market for casual games will exceed 2 billion dollars in the U.S. alone" (Kuittinen, et al., 2007, p. 105).

There are several factors and requirements for the development of digital casual games. Most of the digital casual games require platforms such as Abobe Flash Player, HTML 5, Java, Mac OS X Leopard or Unity (Cheng, 2011). Usually, a game is created by several different groups of people. These development teams include designers, artists, programmers, level designers, sounds engineers and testers. Game mechanics are at the core of digital casual games, according to Cheng (2011). For instance, players are able to create matches of three items, such as in Candy Crush Saga. To avoid players from becoming frustrated and dropping the game it is very important that the mechanisms work perfectly. Mechanics are seen as most important with regard to successful gameplay (Cheng, 2011).

The games can be played via various platforms such as personal computers (including Facebook), various consoles, tablets and mobile phones. They are nonviolent, arcade-style games that involve puzzles, words, board and card games, game show and trivia. As mentioned before, digital casual games are assumed to be produced for the general public and families. Therefore these games do not only fit perfectly into young people's lives but also busy adults' lifes (Cheng, 2011). Mobile platforms emphasise the "anytime, anywhere" attitude concerning digital casual games. However, it might be that *casual* is not so casual anymore. Casual game players play a lot more than initially thought (Kuittinen et al., 2007). However, even though this sector is targeting the mass market, 61% of players are over the age of 35 (Clark, 2007). Kuittinen et al. (2007) support these results by confirming that the majority of players are middle-aged and older women. Soh and Tan (2008) argue that this is the case because men prefer games that contain shooting, sports and other action-game genres. Women, on the other hand, prefer to play puzzle and role-playing games, according to Soh and Tan (2008).

Common elements in the design of digital casual games have been found. They should have a clear goal and objective, outcome and feedback, conflict, competition, challenge and opposition and interaction according to Schwabe and Goth (2005). Cheng (2011) supports these elements and adds the following elements: 1) rules and roles must be clear; 2) players need to be able to quickly reach proficiency; 3) casual gameplay adapts to a players' life and schedule; and 4) game concepts borrow familiar content and themes from life. Finally, the game should also be innovative (Shelley, 2001). The most popular digital casual games have all these elements, however this does not mean that the elements made the games successful. Not only the way a game is designed matters for the path to 'success'.

Another aspect of the path to success is the following question: why do people play digital casual games. According to Di Loreto and Gouaich (2010) the basic motivation to play social digital casual games comes from the relationship between the psychological needs of the user and the social gaming situations. The authors used Murray's categories of psychological needs to assess the motivation for playing such games. In addition, their results showed that the most popular digital casual games included the following needs: 1) gift your friends; 2) share your wealth; 3) challenge your friends; 4) highscores of friends and world; 5) ask your friend to use the app; 6) list of friends already using the app; 7) helping friends; and 8) notifications. Including these elements will not necessarily result in an increase of popularity, however these elements appear to be preferred by the audience.

Another way to measure why people want to play a casual game is through the Technology Acceptance Model (TAM) (Ha, Yoon, & Choi, 2007). This model can explain 80% of game playing (Hsu & Lu, 2007) and is easy to apply (Mathieson, 1991). Perceived usefulness and perceived ease of use have been shown to be factors in explaining user acceptance behavior toward a system and especially in mobile game users. It has been proven that perceived usefulness did not motivate users to play online games, but directly affected user attitude. To measure this variable, the authors looked at ease of use, self-expression, visibility and innovativeness. Mathieson (1991) compared the TAM model to other models such as the Theory of Planned Behavior and concluded that the TAM model is easier to apply. With TAM

10

researchers are able to identify dissatisfied consumers and discover the nature of their complaints. People usually just want to kill time (Hsu & Lu, 2004) when they play digital casual games. However, it is important to keep the customers loyal to your product, as companies still want their consumers to play even though they have a very busy life and thus have no time to kill. The TAM model can also investigate factors that are essential to loyalty. Especially for digital casual games it is important to keep the players loyal to the game. With Angry Bird, Candy Crush Saga and Flappy Bird players can download the free demo version first, which is used to gain trust and to start a relationship. Digital casual games are often marketed with the "try before you buy model", which holds that consumers get the option to download the demo version for free first (Kuittinen, 2007). This means that you can try a game first before you have to pay for the full version.

The most common business models (Kuittinen et al., 2007) are: 1) try and buy downloadables; 2) advertising sponsored; and 3) in-game micro-payments. In-game micro-payments are often used in digital casual games nowadays. For example, in Candy Crush Saga you can buy extra lives or superpowers to obtain the next level. It concerns small amounts, such as 99 cents. A lot of digital casual games now also make use of push messages or notifications that pop up on the screen of smartphones (Scharl, Dickinger, & Murphy, 2005). The game will then send a push message when you have new lives or when a new action is available. In addition, some games also send the users a reminder when they have not been playing the game for a while. These notifications can be perceived as spam, which is an issue for the developers that try to engage the gamers to play the games again. Because of this Scharl, Dickinger and Murphy (2005) point out that the message should contain the right content, it should be personalized and the users should have control over the notifications. Finally, the message should be readable on any platform.

Another way to advertise the game is through advergames or in-game advertising (Winkler & Buckner, 2006). Both Winkler and Buckner (2006) and Purswani (2010) define advergames as online games designed with the purpose to promote a certain brand. Companies need interactive gaming technology to deliver embedded advertising messages to the customer in online games. Winkler and Buckner (2006) also argue that digital casual games are often

11

affiliated with advergames, web games and downloadable games. However, the authors conclude that advergames might not work effectively for brands that are already known to the game player. In addition, the majority of participants from their survey sample (80 individuals) were negative about advertising in games. Nonetheless, this finding does not change the fact that the respondents still prefer to play free casual games. This means that the trial version with advertisements is preferred instead of paying for the complete game without advertisements.

According to Michael Pachter of Wedbush Morgan Securities as cited in Kuittinen et al. (2007, p. 108) "casual games will be a big part of the overall growth but they will not dominate the future." However, research by Informa Media Group as cited in Soh and Tan (2008, p. 37) suggested that "by 2010 mobile gaming will overtake both console and personal computer gaming in terms of market value." Now, digital casual games changed the game industry. There used to be only a few game developers whereas now there are many developers trying to focus on various platforms.

An important theory to look at when conducting this case study research is the product life cycle theory (PLC). According to Rink and Swan (1979) this theory represents the unit sales curve for a product from when it was launched until it is removed, looking at four different stages. First, the introduction where the sales are low since only few consumers know about the product. Secondly, the growth where consumers recognize and accept the product after which the sales start to increase. Thirdly, the maturity where more competitors appear and the growth will ease off. Finally, a decline in sales will occur (Rink & Swan, 1979). The process of experimentation of the product eventually leads to a dominant design (Funk, 2004). Therefore, the only assets companies can distinguish themselves with are marketing, distribution and after-sales support. Angry Birds, Candy Crush Saga and Flappy Bird can be analyzed best by looking at it from this theory, as it identifies four different stages of the path to success.

The PLC theory has been formulated as an "explicit, verifiable model of sales behavior" (Polli & Cook, 1969, p. 400). In addition, the theory was tested in 140 categories of goods and has proven to be valuable in understanding the process of consumer goods use and acceptance. According to Polli and Cook (1969) the theory can be useful for marketing planning and sales forecasting. However, Day (1981) stated a lot of people within the marketing field have different opinions about this theory. The theory has great value when used as a framework for explaining market dynamics (Day, 1981). Various factors have been tested to influence the sequence and duration of the stages of the PLC theory but all of them were not significant. Therefore, the theory cannot be used to anticipate changes.

Taking all the literature into consideration for this research, it is important to specify which terms and aspects of the theory will be focused on most. This study investigates *the process of 'success' for the development of digital casual games and the implications of this 'success'.*

Digital casual games are seen as quick to access, easy to learn and with no game experience required. For this research, it is important to investigate how the digital casual games Angry Birds, Candy Crush Saga and Flappy Bird have developed. Therefore, the elements that Schwabe and Goth (2005) and Cheng (2011) agreed upon will be used: 1) rules and roles must be clear; 2) players need to be able to quickly reach proficiency; 3) casual gameplay adapts to a players' life and schedule; and 4) game concepts borrow familiar content and themes from life. These aspects will be examined for each case study's process of success as they can identify the strategic decisions that companies or developers made. Next to the elements of Schwabe and Goth (2005) and Cheng (2011), this research will draw from the product life cycle theory. By using the four stages of the product life cycle theory and looking at the elements of Angry Birds, Candy Crush Saga and Flappy Bird, the relationship and the notion of success will be examined in the present research.

Chapter 3: Method

This research focuses on the process of 'success' for the development of digital casual games and the implications of this 'success'. It does so by looking at these three games: Angry Birds, Candy Crush Saga and Flappy Bird. This research also looks at the relationship between these digital casual games and social media. Little research has been done on the subject of marketing and digital casual games, which is why this research is relevant to conduct. Even though this specific subject has not been researched, this research will built on the structure of previous case study researches. According to Cambell and Ahrens (1998) case study research is conducted combined with interviews, surveys or document analysis.

3.1 Research method

Case study as a research method is often indexed as neither quantitative nor qualitative (Zucker, 2009). This methodology was chosen with a qualitative approach, which enables in-depth analyses. Documents of three cases were analyzed from a certain time period, to identify the path to success and thus the choices companies made. The aim of this research is not to find out why digital casual games can become successful, but rather what the specific path of each of the three digital casual games was to successfulness and the implications of this 'success'.

3.2 Case selection

The cases were selected by looking at only one factor: the digital casual games should be in the top 10 games in the Apple store and on Google Play. This is because when a game is selected to be in the top 10 games, it must be popular and thus successful. Using these predetermined criteria the following digital casual games were chosen: Angry Birds, Candy Crush Saga and Flappy Bird. Analyzing three cases would be more compelling than focusing on only one case (Meyer, 2001), since they all have different histories and production and are seen as exemplary forms of casual game success.

Candy Crush Saga is digital casual game developed by King. This game is focused on a sweet and colorful world of candy, where users have to mix and match sweets in combination of three or more. Candy Crush Saga is also available through Facebook, Android and iOS devices. Angry Birds was developed by Rovio Entertainment in 2003. This puzzle game has been turned into a brand and now offers numerous games: Angry Birds Seasons, Angry Birds Rio, Angry Birds Space, Angry Birds Friends, Amazing Alex, Bad Piggies, Angry Birds Star Wars, Angry Birds Star Wars II and Angry Birds GO! In the game, users shoot various types of birds (with powers) towards pigs with a catapult, the bad guys, and the houses they live in. Finally, Flappy Bird was developed by Dong Nguyen and produced by GEARS Studios. This game was only available for a short period of time, as Dong Nguyen eventually deleted it from game stores for reasons that will be discussed later on. In this game the user plays as a bird and by tapping the screen the bird has to flap through different lengths of pipes.

3.3 Data collection and analysis

For this research, data was collected through online desk research including English news articles and blogs, which can be split into blog articles and blog reviews. These sources were selected with the help of the following search terms: 1) candy crush saga; 2) angry birds; and 3) flappy bird. This was because all data was treated equally. However, using these search terms resulted in an extremely large amount of data and the top results only showed articles from May 2014. The search term 'candy crush saga' yielded 40,200,000 results. The search term 'angry birds' provided 140,000,000 results and finally the search term 'flappy bird' gave 83,200,000 results. Therefore, a more systemic approach was necessary. Within Google there was an option to set a timeframe and consequently, this narrowed the search down. With regard to Candy Crush this study analyzed articles from the years 2012, 2013 and 2014. For Angry Birds articles from the years 2009 until 2014 were selected. Finally, for Flappy Bird articles from the years 2013 and 2014 were analyzed. For all individual cases, each year was split into two periods of six months whereby articles were selected based upon top results. This way it was possible to take the top results, since the results only showed data that was highly ranked in that time period. Three pages of top results were checked and some articles were skimmed to check whether they could be relevant to this research. In the end, articles from various news outlets were selected such as The Guardian, BBC News, The New York Times, The Economist, Business Insider and Forbes. With regard to the cases, Angry Birds ended up with 18 articles, Candy Crush Saga with 19 articles and finally Flappy Bird with 20 articles.

First the data with regard to Angry Birds were analyzed and coded, after which the data for Candy Crush Saga were analyzed and coded and finally the data for Flappy Bird were analyzed and coded. This "data analysis consists of examining, categorizing, tabulating, or otherwise recombining the evidence to address the initial propositions of a study" (Tellis, 1997). In order to complete this more fully, the data were analyzed with the help of the 30-days trial version of the software program Nvivo 10. Open codes were formed during the analysis of the articles and blogs. During the open coding process this research focused on various aspects of the articles: what is happening, what is important, what patterns emerge and thoughts and ideas. Open or initial coding refers to first impression phrases (Saldana, 2009). According to Saldana (2009) patterns can be characterized by similarities, differences, frequencies, sequences, correspondences and causation. Pieces of text and individual words were highlighted in the articles after which a code was assigned. After the first open coding process, the steps were repeated. This was necessary to select other open codes and to reassess them. They were refined, expanded, uncoded, merged, split and/or rejected. The final list of 35 open codes formed the coding frame of this research. Angry Birds ended up with 16 open codes, Candy Crush Saga with 14 open codes and Flappy Bird with 15 open codes.

For the last step of the coding process axial codes or categories needed to be appointed (Saldana, 2009). These categories or codes serve as an umbrella for open codes. The above process was repeated exactly the same with regard to every case. An overview of all the open and axial codes can be found in the appendixes. The axial codes were chosen because they relate perfectly to this research and its main question. In addition, the codes depicture a chronological process of the success. The axial and open codes with regard to Angry Birds are: Rovio (strategy, previous games, bankruptcy, employees and competition), Angry Birds (game design, compatibility and usage), perception of success (financial success, game design, community, users, compatibility and in top), way to success (strategy, compared to other games, compatibility and usage) and implications of success (addiction, privacy issue and future). The axial codes for Candy Crush Saga are: King (strategy, employees and previous games), Candy Crush Saga (game design and usage), perception of success (financial success, game design, community, users and in top), way to success (strategy, compatibility and compared to other games) and implications of success (addiction, trademarks, competition and future). Finally, the axial codes for Flappy Bird are: Dong Nguyen (previous games), Flappy Bird (game design, compared to other games, compatibility and usage), perception of success (financial success, game design, in top, users and community), way to success (strategy, compared to other games and compatibility) and implications of success (future, addiction, pull plug).

Each data source was analyzed independently but not treated independently, meaning that while reading an article the information was immediately connected to other data in an attempt to understand the overall case (Baxter & Jack, 2008).

Chapter 4: Results

4.1 Case 1: Angry Birds

An article in The Telegraph argued that Rovio, the creator of Angry birds, had drawn up a make-or-break business plan involving Apple's iPhone (Kendall, 2011). Rovio had to make this plan work since they were close to bankruptcy in 2009 (Cheshire, 2011). However, first a design for the game had to be made. In the same year, a game designer at Rovio named Jaakko Iisalo was thinking about the project he had been set at work. He already submitted a number of ideas that had been rejected by the directors for being too complicated, simplistic or boring. Iisalo switched to Photoshop and started designing round birds without legs, with thick eyebrows and with crazed expressions on their face. "I didn't think it was special at the time," stated Iisalo (Kendall, 2011). However, when he presented the screenshot to Niklas Hed, chief executive officer at Rovio, it caused quite the commotion. "People saw this picture and it was just magical," argued Hed, "As soon as I saw those characters I liked them. Straight away, I had a feeling that I wanted to play the game." Iisalo made the birds angry because players can smash them into things and it's OK; if the birds would look cute it would repulse people (Wortham, 2010).

Rovio had created 50 games before Angry Birds and when the iPhone came out in 2007 Rovio knew what aspects to take into account and what to look out for due to notes from focus groups it had organized over the years (Kendall, 2011). Rovio realized that their industry was about to change; users would be able to download games from the same place, namely Apple's App Store. This also meant that only one version of the game has to be made, which reduced the costs enormously. The focus groups were held over the years during which Rovio employees "watched people playing games from behind a glad screen and recorded what the players found difficult, what excited them and what they found boring" (Kendall, 2011). This resulted in a blueprint of the "perfect" game. The main things Rovio has gotten from these focus groups are that levels should be achievable and the game should be playable in a coffee-break. These principles led to the design of Angry Birds. According to Rovio, players had to know immediately what to do in a game. This was the reason why Rovio choose the catapult, the main feature in Angry Birds. People instinctively know how to use a catapult.

When playing Angry Birds, several different backgrounds and different birds are visible. On the left side of the smartphone screen are the birds, which you must launch through the air at the pigs using a catapult, which can be handled with only one finger. Players can score points by destroying the forts and 'squashing' the pigs. The trajectories differ in every level and some birds are more effective than others. There are seven main types of birds according to the Angry Birds website (Rovio, 2014): 1) Red – does great at popping pigs; 2) The Blues – splits into three smaller birds; 3) Chuck – picks up speed and distance; 4) Bomb – explodes; 5) Matilda – drops an egg bomb; 6) Terence – destroys everything easily and 7) Bubbles – inflates to a huge size. When players hit the pigs' shelters in the right place with the right bird, they are generously rewarded with points.

Rovio also had a strategy for getting to the top of the iPhone chart. Hed believed that Rovio needed a strong brand to put a face to their product (Kendall, 2011), "We looked at the App Store and realized the power of the brand." However, Rovio cannot take all the credit for this strategy. Chillingo, a company which had good contacts at Apple and had made unknown brands No 1, published Angry Birds.

Rovio first invested 100,000 euros to develop Angry Birds, but it was an investment that paid off. Angry Birds already had a turnover of 50 million euros in 2011 alone (Cheshire, 2011). In 2010, Apple stated that it was the best-selling iPhone app of that year. The free versions produced $1 million a month in advertising revenue by the end of 2010. Since the launch of the game with 63 levels in December 2009, Rovio has added another 147 levels. Angry Birds saved Rovio from going bankrupt just in time. The game became so popular that they also released themed versions at Halloween, Christmas and Valentine in 2010. In the same year, the game inspired people and homemade Angry Birds costumes became big hits on Halloween. Conan O'Brien demonstrated the game on YouTube and celebrities such as Justin Bieber showed their love for Angry Birds on social networks. Angry Birds became hyped, with 50 million downloads

19

in 2010 (Wortham, 2010) and 648 million downloads in 2012 (Olson, 2012). According to an article in the Guardian (Dredge, 2012), in the end of 2012 the game was being used by 200 million monthly active players

Rovio is currently working on an Angry Birds 3D movie that is expected to launch in 2016 (Dredge, 2012). The company has set its eyes on Hollywood as it has also been announced that Rovio will bring Angry Birds Star Wars to the next-gen consoles, which means that a video game will be launched on the Xbox One (Moore, 2013). According to an article in The Telegraph (Kendall, 2011) Rovio no longer sees itself as games developer, but rather as a media company focused on building strong brands. The soft toys, phone cases, comics and the movie are all planned. In 2014, Rovio revealed that they are working on an adventure role-playing game, which will be available for iOS, Android and Windows Phone 8 (Fahey, 2014). According to an article in the Business Insider, CMO Pete Vesterbacka revealed that Rovio wants to emulate Disney (Smith, 2014).

4.1.1 Discussion
Cheng (2011) mentioned the following common elements in the design of digital casual games: 1) rules and roles must be clear; 2) players need to able to quickly reach proficiency; 3) casual gameplay adapts to a players' life and schedule; and 4) game concepts borrow familiar content and themes from life. Firstly, the rules are not specifically told or shown in Angry Birds, because Rovio wanted players to instinctively know what to do. This refers back to the choice of using the catapult. The roles are not made clear, as it is part of the game to find out which bird is most useful in a certain situation. Secondly, players are able to quickly reach proficiency as operating the game is easy. No game experience is needed to understand how to use the controls: the game can be played with only one finger. Thirdly, the gameplay adapts to a players' life and schedule due to the fact that the game is compatible for various devices. For instance, one could start playing at home on the computer and then on their way to work by using their smartphone. Finally, the game borrows familiar content and themes from life as

Angry Birds makes use of the birds, the pigs and the catapult. Even though these aspects do not reflect real life, they were the foundation of the design.

To connect the above findings with the research question and the product life cycle theory, one must see the development of Angry Birds in chronological order. Rovio made up a make-or-break-it plan as they were about to go bankrupt. With the help of focus groups they knew what aspects to integrate and when the right design came up they launched their game. Rovio had a plan for their way to success and asked Chillingo to publish the game through the App Store because of their good contacts with Apple. These steps were all part of the introduction stage. The game became immensely popular and brought in great revenue. Unfortunately, the cause of the popularity has not been found. Social media was not used to launch their game or to provide extra promotion. These steps belong to the growth stage. Now, Rovio wants to become a word brand and has already made quite some merchandise, such as soft toys. In 2016 Rovio will launch their first Angry Birds movie. Their goal is to become a media company with a strong brand. Angry Birds is still in the maturity stage, which means that the original game is still in the top 10 (see Figure 1).

Stage	Happenings	Actions
1. Introduction	Make-it-break it plan	Design game, focus groups, App Store, Angry Birds
2. Growth	Hype	New level, other versions, App Store, Google Play
3. Maturity	Community	Angry Birds movie, merchandise, world brand
4. Decline	-	-

Figure 1

Finally, according to Shelly (2011) the term success is often referred to in numbers, such as the revenue of the number of downloads, ranking and users. In this case, success was indeed frequently referred to in numbers. However looking at the bigger picture, Rovio has climbed its way to the top with the help of various strategies and great game design.

4.2 Case 2: Candy Crush Saga

February 2014, Candy Crush Saga's creator King was being accused by the creator of CandySwipe, who claimed that the company was taking the food out of his family's mouth (GameCentral, 2014). Candy Crush Saga became amazingly popular and as a part of King's strategy the words 'candy' and 'saga' were trademarked. This decision was purposeful and intended to secure some of their success within various gaming platforms. This made it difficult for other developers who had similar games, or similar names of games, because they could not use either of these words without facing legal action from King. CandySwipe is a game available on Apple and Android devices wherein, just as in Candy Crush Saga, candy is crushed for points. However, CandySwipe made use of different kinds of candy and the ways to crush them. The creator of CandySwipe attempted to trademark the name of his game; however King argued that this game was a clone of Candy Crush Saga (GameCentral, 2014), despite the fact that CandySwipe came out two years before. It got even worse, since King and the creator of CandySwipe were both trying to buy the rights to an earlier game called Candy Crusher. Eventually, King owned the rights to this game and thus became the original trademark holder of everything video game and candy-related. The creator of CandySwipe sued King but conceded. Albert Ransom, president of Runsome Apps wrote a letter to King explaining how he felt about the situation (GameCentral, 2014):

"Good for you, you win. I hope you're happy taking the food out of my family's mouth when CandySwipe clearly existed well before Candy Crush Saga. I wanted to take this moment to write you this letter so that you know who I am. Because I now know exactly what you are. Congratulations on your success! Sincerely, Albert Ransom, President (Founder), Runsome Apps Inc."

It has not only been CandySwipe and its creator that has been affected by King's tactics. Stoic, another game developer has been prevented from using 'Saga' in their game's title (Kain, 2014). The game is funded through Kickstarter and only available via STEAM, which is a software platform that distributes pc games. The game is inspired by Viking legend and makes players re-

22

experience classic adventures and tactics. King stated that they were not trying to stop Banner Saga from using its name. They just wanted to protect their image, since now any developer can say that their 'Saga' game is legitimate, which holds that it is part of King's Saga games. This is of great importance to King, since 'Saga' is the key of association with the company. Stoic noted that their trademark application predates King's trademark application; however the problem was that King could easily start a legal fight since they are financially strong and Stoic would go bankrupt trying to protect its game (Kain, 2014). Stoic's game The Banner Saga had absolutely nothing to do with Candy Crush Saga, but King is ready to threaten every game with legal action that comes even close to their creation. King is one of the most successful companies nowadays, but how did King's Candy Crush Saga become so successful?

King is a British company that started developing games in 2003 with a team of 150 employees that expanded to around 550 employees in 2013 (Dredge, 2013). Palm, a designer at King's, argued in an article by Dredge (2013) that their "core focus is definitely on casual social games, but we want to keep on experimenting and pushing the envelope." These casual social games can be found on personal computers (including through Facebook as a platform), iOS devices and Android devices.

Bubble Saga was one of the earlier games of King, where players had to shoot bubbles to create groups of three or more to make them burst. When all the bubbles are gone the game is over. With this game King tried various approaches to Facebook. It turned out that the Saga formula was successful (Osborne, 2012). When King found the right approach to Facebook, they launched their old game Candy Crush Saga in April 2012 (Tam, 2013). Even though the game already existed, it became enormously popular on Facebook after its launch. This change of events caused great brand awareness for King. The year 2013 "has been one of the most exciting times for King" was argued by Palm. In addition, an article on BBC News (2013) indicated that Sebastian Knutsson, chief creative officer and co-founder of King, and his team did not expect the success of Candy Crush Saga when developing the game. King's strategy includes focusing a lot on player experience, and they do not differentiate between people who pay and who don't – "we just see them as players and optimize in making the game is really fun," argues Palm.

Candy Crush Saga is a candy-themed puzzle where players have to match as many identical pieces of candy with a limited number of moves. Every time players pass a level, the next one gets more difficult. They can unlock more levels by inviting their friends via Facebook and purchase in-game items. According to Appdata, which tracks application usage statistics, this game has more than 45 million monthly players (Tam, 2013) and it was featured in the video clip of Psy's new hit: Gangnam Style. It had 100 million daily active users across all its web and mobile games (Dredge, 2013).

In 2012, King's Chief Marketing Officer Dale revealed to Seufert (2013) that in-app advertising accounted for 15% of King's overall revenue. One year later King announced that it would discontinue its mobile advertising efforts. Instead, they would only focus on revenue from in-app purchases. King stated that "King's #1 focus around delivering an uninterrupted entertainment experience for our network of loyal players across web, tablet and mobile has unfortunately led to the difficult decision of removing advertising as a core element of King's overall strategy" (Dano, 2013). The in-app purchases are estimated to come close to $900,000 per day (Dockterman, 2013). Thus even though Candy Crush Saga can be downloaded for free, King makes money from the in-app purchases of extra moves, lives and power-ups. Dredge (2013) claimed that only 30% who've reached the final level have not paid for in-app purchases. In addition, Candy Crush Saga is regularly updated, however if players get bored King hopes they move on to one of the other Saga's. It appears this strategy is working, though it has some significant risks. Another plan they followed was Facebook and word-of-mouth marketing. King did not spend a ton of money on marketing but let their fans do the work. However, in the end of 2013 King was investing in a TV ad campaign for the game (Elliss, 2013). King did not indicate the reasons for why the campaign was launched.

Apple praised the game as most downloaded free app of 2013 (Vincent, 2014). King revealed that they have 70 million daily active users across all platforms. In May, Candy Crush had passed Farmville's developer Zygna, who had 52 million daily active users. In 2009, it was the most popular game on Facebook and since then Zygna experienced a decline. Candy Crush Saga however, has been played 700 million times a day on smartphones and tablets according to an article in the Guardian (Dredge, 2013). Out of these 700 million players, 132.4 million players have connected to the game to Facebook. Again, this statement was supported by AppData (MacMillan & Spears, 2013) which claimed that Candy Crush Saga has become the most popular game played on Facebook with more than 45 million users. According to an article on BBC News (2013) this game became so popular because players can start a game over breakfast, on the train and at work. This means that they can continue their game where they left off on any device.

King is currently working on the next game in the Saga series: Papa Pear Saga. An article in The Guardian (Dredge, 2013) stated that Palm argued "we want to take games to where the players are, and right now, the players are on PCs, Android and iOS." Palm revealed that consoles are not on the radar for now, since they do not have enough numbers there.

4.2.1 Discussion

Cheng (2011) mentioned the following common elements in the design of digital casual games: 1) rules and roles must be clear; 2) players need to able to quickly reach proficiency; 3) casual gameplay adapts to a players' life and schedule; and 4) game concepts borrow familiar content and themes from life. Firstly, the rules and roles are shown in Candy Crush Saga, because the game shows what candy-mixes result in special powers. In addition, the game also explains how to give extra lives to friends and how to invite friends to play the game. Secondly, players are able to quickly reach proficiency as operating the game is easy. No game experience is needed to understand how to use the controls: the game can be played with only one finger. Thirdly, the gameplay adapts to a players' life and schedule due to the fact that the game is compatible for various devices. For instance, one could start playing at home on the computer and then on their way to work by using their smartphone. Finally, the game borrows familiar content and themes from life as Candy Crush Saga makes use of different kinds of candy. Even though this aspect does not reflect real life, candy is the foundation of the design.

Now the development of the game is clear, the strategic actions of King are identified through the product life cycle theory. The process of success for Candy Crush Saga started with the first Saga game, which was part of the introduction stage of the product life cycle theory. King tried a couple of approaches to Facebook and decided to launch Candy Crush Saga on that platform in 2012. After financial success, King removed all the in-app advertisements in 2013 and only focused on in-app purchases for revenue. This was also to improve the gameplay for the users. During the second stage, Candy Crush Saga became extremely popular since their launch on Facebook and in the maturity stage, King applied for the trademarks on the words 'candy' and 'saga'. In addition, King has started with broadcasting TV advertisement to capitalize on their success with exposure, as they want to make a whole Saga series of games. They want to make a Saga brand and become even greater. Candy Crush Saga, just as Angry Birds, is still a top 10 game according to the data (see Figure 2).

Stage	Happenings	Actions
1. Introduction	Saga plan	First Saga game, approaches with Facebook, Candy Crush Saga
2. Growth	Hype	Remove in-app ads, new levels, other Saga games, Facebook, App Store, Google Play
3. Maturity	Community	Trademarks, TV ads, Saga series
4. Decline	-	-

Figure 2

Finally, success is referred to in terms of revenue, ranking and downloads/users again. However, different from Angry Birds, King used Facebook to launch Candy Crush Saga and this led to big success.

4.3 Case 3: Flappy Bird

Dong Nguyen, the creator of Flappy Bird, is still making money even though the game was pulled out of the App Store and Google Play. People who still have the app on their device and play it result in revenue for the creator (Rigney, 2014). Even though Flappy Bird cannot be downloaded anymore, the Flappy Bird players are fighting to bring it back. There is a 'Save Flappy Bird' Twitter account, which had more than 2,000 followers. This account still exists, however now that the hype passed and Dong Nguyen is busy with other games, the numbers followers decreased to 566 (see picture 1). In addition, the hashtag #RIPFlappyBird was being used on Twitter all over the world. A lot of people were shocked and showed their respect when the game was pulled, including the world famous YouTube star PewDiePie (see picture 2). PewDiePie or Felix Arvid Ulf Kjellberg is a Swedish commentator of video games with more than 26 million followers.

Figure 3   Figure 4

Flappy Bird is a very simplistic casual game. Players have to tap the smartphone screen to make the bird flap. They have to try not to hit any of the green pipes, as this ends the game. The goal is to obtain the highest score possible. Dong Nguyen, creator of Flappy Bird, became fascinated by the possibilities of the touch screen on the iPhone. He based the game on Nintendo games of his youth such as super Mario Bros with its iconic green pipes. In addition, the game should be playable on the move and thus the game should be played with one hand. He developed the game in only a few nights (Hamburger, 2014).

Flappy Bird was launched on Apple's App Store on the 24th of May 2013. It moved up in their rankings within the family game category, after which its place in the rankings dropped again. On the 29th of October 2013 the game was back in the charts. Flappy Bird had several massive download bursts within 24 hours and with each burst the game climbed higher up the charts. After this, a sharp decrease in ranking took place and a burst kicked in right on time again. This went on until the 17th of January 2014. One of the first tweets the creator received was: "I hate you and your stupid fucking game! I mean I hit one feather on a pipe and die! How realistic is that?!?" Dong Nguyen replied with: "Please don't expect realistic in games. Besides, I think my games are not for everybody." Since the end of January, the creator had replied to dozens of gamers, addressing buys, explaining the medal system and laughing off the angry tweets (Mosendz, 2014). From September 2013 until February 2014, Flappy Bird was the No. 1. free app on Apple's App Store. By February, the game was being played in more than 100 countries and had been downloaded more than 50 million times (Kushner, 2014). In addition, it had more than 47.000 reviews in the App Store (Hamburger, 2014). Since the creator did not use any promotion methods, the game seemed based on word-of-mouth marketing according to The Atlantic (Rigney, 2014). "I didn't use any promotion methods. All accounts on Twitter, Facebook and Instagram about Flappy Bird are not mine. The popularity could be my luck," was argued by an article in The Guardian (Dredge, 2014). In addition, Flappy Bird got recommended by Youtube's biggest star PewDiePie, an influential Swedish gamer. The video has been watched more than 8.1 million times. Even Apple has shared their high score of 99 with their Twitter account (Dredge, 2014).

As the number of users/downloads increased, Dong Nguyen was reported to be making $50,000 per day in ad revenue (NativeX, 2013). Flappy Bird was a free game, no strings attached. There were no in-app advertisements and no in-app purchases. The money Nguyen made was due to unobtrusive advertising (Mc Shea, 2014). Games using this kind of advertising are very common in the Japanese market (Hamburger, 2014).

Another consequence of the increase in users/downloads was that the creator received a lot of threats and people started to look critical towards the game. The idea seems to be copied from other games as the art and sound effects are taken from Super Mario Bros (Tassi, 2014). According to an article in The Guardian (Dredge, 2014), Nguyen started to tweet about his success: "cannot take this anymore", "struggling to cope with its success". Therefore, it was not a surprise when he decided to take the game down. Nguyen argued that it had nothing to do with legal issues. The most famous tweet holds: "I am sorry 'Flappy Bird' users, 22 hours from now; I will take 'Flappy Bird' down. I cannot take this anymore." After this tweet, he went silent for a while even though the majority of his 45.000 followers were trying to contact him (Tassi, 2014). The creator told many newspapers and magazines that he could not take the success anymore, he could not sleep. On Sunday the 9th of February at 12 PM United States time he took the game down.

Due to the popularity of Flappy Bird, a community of fans has formed and they will not stop hoping for the return of Flappy Bird. In a recent interview (Kelly, 2014) Nguyen confirms that there will be a next version, but different and even better. He finally states that he is not interested in selling Flappy Bird and that he still makes games. This means that even though Flappy Bird made his life miserable, he still achieved big success with the game.

4.3.1 Discussion

Cheng (2011) mentioned the following common elements in the design of digital casual games: 1) rules and roles must be clear; 2) players need to able to quickly reach proficiency; 3) casual gameplay adapts to a players' life and schedule; and 4) game concepts borrow familiar content and themes from life. Firstly, the rules are shown with the help of the sign 'tap to flap the bird up and down' when starting the game. The roles are not clear in Flappy Bird, as the game does not have a narrative like Angry Birds or Candy Crush Saga. Secondly, players are able to quickly reach proficiency as operating the game is easy. No game experience is needed to understand how to use the controls: the game can be played with only one finger. Thirdly, the gameplay adapts to a players' life and schedule due to the fact that the game is compatible for various devices. For instance, one could start playing at home on the computer and then on their way to work by using their smartphone. Finally, the game borrows familiar content and themes from life as Flappy Bird makes use of the bird. Even though this aspect does not reflect real life, the bird is the foundation of the game.

Flappy bird was a unique case, since Dong Nguyen did not plan on the game to become so successful when he launched the game on the App store during the introduction stage. He had hoped that this would happen though, however his success became too much. He pulled the game from the App Store and Google Play in February, 2014 during the growth stage. After that, many fans fought to get the game back. After a few months, these followers stopped fighting for the game in the decline stage (see Figure 5). Flappy Bird has not been in the maturity stage, as the game was only available for a short period. There were no other levels or versions made by the creator. Currently, the @SaveFlappyBird account on Twitter only has around 600 followers left out of the 2000. Nguyen stated that he is working on a different and better version; however this version will not be launched soon. In the meantime, he is busy developing other games.

Stage	Happenings	Actions
1. Introduction	Simple game	App Store, rankings up and down
2. Growth	Hype & removal	Pulled from App Store and Google Play, working on other games, maybe in the future a different and better version
3. Decline	Community	@SaveFlappyBird account decrease, other games

Figure 5

Finally, in this case, success is referred to in numbers again. Different than Angry Birds and Candy Crush Saga, Flappy Bird became partially famous through Twitter. He had all contact with fans and media through this medium about the game. After the game was pulled, Twitter accounts and hashtags were used to fight and to bring the game back.

Chapter 5: Conclusion

This research studied the *process of 'success' for the development of digital casual games and the implications of this 'success'*. Specifically, the study concentrated on the digital casual games Angry Birds, Candy Crush Saga and Flappy Bird. The research question was divided in three parts: the process of success, the implications and the relationship of digital casual games with social media. Before these three aspects could be handled, case study research had to be conducted. The findings have shown that the process of success and its implications differ per case. For case 1, Angry Birds, the process was highlighted by the make-or-break business plan, their focus groups research, the design and their plan to rank No 1 in the App Store. The implications of its success hold that Rovio wants to become a world brand with all the merchandise they have produced, such as soft toys. For case 2, Candy Crush Saga, the process was highlighted by the Saga games, Facebook, the trademarks, in-app purchases and the design. The implications of its success hold that King has started with broadcasting TV ads to get to capitalize on their success. Next to that, they also want to promote their other Saga games. For case 3, Flappy Bird, the process was highlighted by the simplicity of the game, threats via Twitter, pulling the game from stores and the fight to get the game back. The implications of its success hold that Dong Nguyen now has a lot of fans but he does not want to bring the game back yet. However, as stated in the research, he is working on a different and better version of the game.

The findings also answered whether there is relationship between social media and the digital casual games. In case 1 there was no relationship. However, case 2 and 3 showed a relationship between social media and the games. For case 2, the game was launched on Facebook and benefited from the users on this platform. With regard to case 3, the developer Dong Nguyen kept contact with his fans this way and later received threats from them. These threats on Twitter caused the game to be removed. The game was a trending topic with the hashtag #RIPFlappyBird. In this case, both parties benefit from the relationship.

These digital casual games support the definition given by Cheng (2011) and Kuittinen et al. (2007): "quick to access, easy to learn and requires no previous special video game skills, expertise of regular time commitment to play" as all three games were based on those aspects. In addition, the three cases also support the statements by Shelley (2001) about success. To describe the success of the games, the revenue, number of downloads and number of users was used. Moreover, this research adds that the ranking is also important when describring the success of digital casual games.

Next to this, the product life cycle theory was drawn upon throughout this research. In the discussion of each game the theory was connected to the collected data. It was remarkable that the four stages of one game compared to another did not have the same duration. This supports what Day (1981) argued in his paper. In addition, the sequence of stages also differed between Flappy Bird and the other games. The theory was useful to analyze the strategic actions of King, Rovio and Dong Nguyen. However, the theory cannot be used to anticipate stages or action as it is too blurry as to where the boundaries of stages are (Polli & Book, 1969). With regard to marketing planning, one can make use of this theory to assess which strategy is most efficient in which stage.

5.1 Limitations and future research

This research gave more insight into the process of success and the implications while looking at Angry Birds, Candy Crush Saga and Flappy Bird. However, the study has some limitations. First of all, the articles for case study research were selected through Google with a timespan of six months. An improvement could be to look into articles from every month, instead of looking for articles from every six months, which was not possible in this research due to time restrictions. Future research should try to get at least one article from every month, to provide a more complete story even though articles will never provide the whole story,. Secondly, the articles were coded by one researcher only, which had some knowledge of these digital casual games already. Future research should have at least two coders when analyzing data, since they might have different interpretations and they could identify different patterns. Thirdly, not all information was available that was needed for these cases. Companies do not share every move they make with regard to strategies and revenues and if they do, they sometimes have a PR manager which only provides a limited and enhanced story to the media. Future research should try to find more sources from the companies themselves, maybe through interviews with the actual developers. Fourthly, the findings from this study cannot be generalized to other digital casual games. However, this is not a problem since many games differ from each other in terms of gameplay, strategy, audience and revenue. Finally, since this research was limited to an amount of data it was not possible to draw a definite cause and effect. Future research should focus on exploring the relationships between certain events. For example, research could focus on the relationship between daily active users and success or in a different light, on whether the top games in the App Store or Google Play have an influence on the company's success – are companies more likely to become successful if their game ranks high?

As little research has been done on the subject of marketing and digital casual games, this paper offers a foundation. In addition, the results of this study give more insight into the processes of Angry Birds, Candy Crush Saga and Flappy Bird which became successful. This information is relevant for people as they need to obtain more knowledge about this topic. The influence of these developers increase, as small companies or even individual designers can turn into big media companies. These media companies will proceed with merchandise and movies next to their games. Finally, people will obtain more knowledge with regard to the kind of digital casual games they are playing and the reasons for the design of the game.

Appendix A: Codes – Angry Birds

Open code	Type of wording used
Financial success	Revenue; profit;
Game design	Mechanics; link to social media;
Strategy	Business model; strategy;
Compared to other games	Compared to; comparison; better; worse; higher; lower
Community	Fans; followers; community
Users	Men; women; different ages
Usage	Coffee-break; not long;
Compatibility	iOS; Android;
Addiction	Addicted; addiction
Privacy issue	Spies; personal data; leaky; user data; privacy; location; NSA or GCHQ programs
Competition	EA games; merge
Future	Soft toys; movie; merchandise;
Employees	Employees Rovio
Bankruptcy	2009; make-or-break it plan;
Previous games	Rovio; other games
In top	Popular; app store; google play; ranking

Open code	Axial code
Financial success; game design; community; users; compatibility; in top	Perception of success
Strategy; compared to other games; compatibility; usage	Way to success
Addiction; privacy issue; future	Implications of success
Strategy; previous games; bankruptcy; employees; competition	Rovio
Game design; compatibility; usage	Angry Birds

Appendix B: Codes – Candy Crush Saga

Open code	Type of wording used
Financial success	Revenue; profit;
Game design	Mechanics; link to social media; features
Strategy	Business model; strategy;
Compared to other games	Compared to; comparison; better; worse; higher; lower
Community	Fans; followers; community
Users	Men; women; different ages
Usage	Coffee-break; not long;
Compatibility	iOS; Android; PC; Facebook
Addiction	Addicted; addiction
Trademarks	Trademarks; Saga; Candy; lawsuits
Competition	Zygna; Farmville
Future	Saga games; TV ads; next level;
Employees	Employees King;
Previous games	King; other games; Saga games
In top	Popular; app store; google play; ranking

Open code	Axial code
Financial success; game design; community; users; in top	Perception of success
Strategy; compatibility; compared to other games	Way to success
Addiction; trademarks; competition; future	Implications of success
Strategy; employees; previous games	King
Game design; usage;	Candy Crush Saga

Appendix C: Codes – Flappy Bird

Open code	Type of wording used
Financial success	Revenue; profit;
Game design	Mechanics; features
Strategy	Business model; strategy; Twitter
Compared to other games	Compared to; comparison; better; worse; higher; lower
In top	Popular; app store; google play; ranking
Community	Fans; followers; community
Users	Men; women; different ages
Usage	Coffee-break; not long;
Compatibility	iOS; Android;
Addiction	Addicted; addiction
Future	Return Flappy Bird; other games; fight for return
Previous games	Dong Nguyen; other games
Pull plug	App Store; Google Play; February 2014; threats; Twitter

Open code	Axial code
Financial success; game design; in top; users; community;	Perception of success
Strategy; compared to other games; compatibility;	Way to success
Future; addiction; pull plug	Implications of success
Previous games	Dong Nguyen
Game design; compared to other games; compatibility; usage	Flappy Bird

Bibliography

Anderson, S. (2012, August 4). Just One More Game. *New York Times*. Retrieved 3 28, 2014, from http://www.nytimes.com/2012/04/08/magazine/angry-birds-farmville-and-other-hyperaddictive-stupid-games.html?pagewanted=all&_r=0

Asur, S., Huberman, B. A., Szabo, G., & Wang, C. (2011). Trends in Social Media: Persistence and Decay. *CoRR*, 434-437.

Baxter, P., & Jack, S. (2008). Qualitative Case Study Methodology: Study Design and Implementation for Novice Researchers. *Qualitative Report, 13*(4), 544-559.

BBC News. (2013, December 18). What is the appeal of Candy Crush Saga? *BBC News*, pp. 1-2.

Bell, M., Chalmers, M., Berkhuus, L., Hall, M., Sherwood, S., Tennent, P., . . . Hampshire, A. (2006). Interweaving Mobile Games with Everyday Life. *Proceedings of the SIGCHI Conference on Human Factors in Computing Systems*, 417-426.

Cambell, R., & Ahrens, C. (1998). Innovative Community Services for Rape Victims: An Application of Multiple Case Study Methodology. *American Journal of Community Psychology, 26*(4), 537-571.

Cheng, K. (2011, January 28). *Casual Gaming*. Retrieved April 11, 2014, from http://www.few.vu.nl/~eliens/project/@archive/vrml-reference/@archive/student/ba-CS/casual-games.pdf

Cheshire, T. (2011, March 7). In depth: How Rovio made Angry Birds a winner (and what's next). *Wired*, pp. 1-3.

Clark, D. (2007). Games, motivation & learning. *Caspian Learning*, 1-22.

Dano, M. (2013, June 12). Candy Crush Saga maker King ditches in-app advertising business. *FierceMobileIT*, pp. 1-2.

Day, G. (1981). The Product Life Cycle: Analysis and Application Issues. *Journal of Marketing, 45*(4), 60-67.

Di Loreto, I., & Gouaich, A. (2010, May 27). *Social Casual Games Success is not so Casual*. Retrieved April 11, 2014, from http://hal.archives-ouvertes.fr/docs/00/48/69/34/PDF/FunAndGames2010-03-22.pdf

Dockterman, E. (2013, November 15). Candy Crush Saga: The Science Behind Our Addiction. *Time*, pp. 1-4.

Dredge, S. (2012, December 11). The Angry Birds Movie Will Be Produced By The Guy Behind 'Despicable Me'. *The Guardian*, pp. 1-2.

Dredge, S. (2013, September 10). Candy Crush Saga: '70% of the people Candy Crush Saga: '70% of the people . *The Guardian*, pp. 1-5.

Dredge, S. (2014, February 8). Flappy Bird at risk of extinction as developer 'cannot take this anymore'. *The Guardian*, pp. 1-3.

Dredge, S. (2014, March 26). Why is Candy Crush Saga so popular? *The Guardian*, pp. 1-4.

Elliss, H. (2013, June 20). Why does Candy Crush Saga need TV ads? *Econsultancy*, pp. 1-2.

Fahey, M. (2014, March 12). The Next Angry Birds Is A Turn-Based Role-Playing Game. *Kotaku*, pp. 1-2.

Funk, J. (2004). The Product Life Cycle Theory and Product Line Management: The Case of Mobile Phones. *Transactions on Engeneering Management, 51*(2), 142-151.

GameCentral. (2014, February 13). Candy Crush Saga makers to sue game they copied. *GameCentral*, pp. 1-4.

Ha, I., Yoon, Y., & Choi, M. (2007). Determinants of adoption of mobile games under mobile broadband wireless access environment. *Information & Management, 44*, 276-286.

Hamburger, E. (2014, February 5). Indie smash hit 'Flappy Bird' racks up $5oK per day in ad revenue. *The Verge*, pp. 1-2.

Hsu, C.-L., & Lu, H.-P. (2004). Who do people play on-line games? An extended TAM with social influences and flow experience. *Information & Management, 41*, 853-868.

Hsu, C.-L., & Lu, H.-P. (2007). Consumer behavior in online game communities: A motivational factor perspective. *Computers in Human Behavior, 23*, 1642-1659.

Kain, E. (2014, January 23). 'Candy Crush Saga' Tries To Crush 'The Banner Saga' In Bizarre Trademark Saga. *Forbes*, pp. 1-4.

Kelly, S. (2014, March 20). 'Flappy Bird' creator confirms next version will be even 'better'. *Mashable*, pp. 1-2.

Kendall, P. (2011, February 7). Angry Birds: the story behind iPhone's gaming phenomenon. *Telegraph*, pp. 1-6.

Kim, H. (2013). Mobile Media Technology And Popular Mobile Game In Contemporary Society. *IJMM 2013, 8*(2), 42-54.

Kuittinen, J., Kultima, A., Niemela, J., & Paavilainen, J. (2007). Casual Games Discussion. *FuturePlay*, 105-110.

Kushner, D. (2014, March 11). The Flight of the Birdman: Flappy Bird Creator Dong Nguyen Speaks Out. *Rolling Stone*, p. 1.

MacMillan, D., & Spears, L. (2013, June 20). 'Candy Crush Saga' Developer Said to Hire Banks for IPO. *Bloomberg*, p. 1.

Mathieson, K. (1991). Predicting User Intentions: Comparing the Technology Acceptance Model with the Theory of Planned Behavior. *Information Systems Research, 2*(3), 173-188.

Mc Shea, T. (2014, February 10). The Rise and Fall of Flappy Bird. *GameSpot*, pp. 1-2.

Meyer, C. (2001). A Case in Case Study Methodology. *Field Methods, 13*(4), 329–352.

Moore, B. (2013, November 1). Would You Pay $50 for Angry Birds on a Next-Gen Console? *Wired Insider*, pp. 1-2.

Mosendz, P. (2014, February 10). Is Your Flappy Bird Phone Now a Collector's Item? *The Wire*, pp. 1-3.

NativeX. (2013, October 29). The Story Behind Why Flappy Bird Was Deleted. *NativeX*, pp. 1-3.

Olson, P. (2012, May 8). A Billionaire Could Queitly Hatch From Angry Birds IPO. *Forbes*, pp. 1-3.

Osborne, J. (2012, April 12). King.com goes for social gamers' sweet tooth with Candy Crush Saga. *Blog Games*, pp. 1-2.

Polli, R., & Cook, V. (1969). Validity of the Product Life Cycle. *Journal of Business, 42*(4), 385-400.

Purswani, G. (2010). Advergames, their use and potential regulation. *Asia Specific Public Relations, 11*, 57-62.

Rigney, R. (2014, February 12). Inside The Brief Life and Untimely Death of Flappy Bird. *Wired Insider*, pp. 1-4.

Rink, D., & Swan, J. (1979). Product Life Cycle Research: A Literature Review. *Journal of Business Research, 7*(3), 219-242.

Rovio. (2014, June 8). *Characters*. Retrieved from Angry Birds: https://www.angrybirds.com/characters

Russoniello, C., O'Brien, K., & Parks, J. M. (2009). The Effectiveness of Casual Video Games in Improving Mood and Decreasing Stress. *Cybertherapy & Rehabilitation, 2*(1), 53-63.

Saldana, J. (2009). An Introduction to Codes and Coding. In J. Saldana, *The coding manual for qualitative researchers* (pp. 1-31). Los Angelos: SAGE.

Scharl, A., Dickinger, A., & Murphy, J. (2005). Diffusion and success factors of mobile marketing. *Electronic Commerce Research and Application, 4*(1), 159-173.

Schwabe, G., & Goth, C. (2005). Mobile learning with a mobile game: design and motivational effects. *Computer Assited Learning, 21*, 204-216.

Seufert, E. (2013, June 17). How much money is Candy Crush Making? *Mobiledevmemo*, pp. 1-3.

Shelley, B. (2001, August 15). Guidelines for Developing Succesful Games. *Gamasutra*. Retrieved April 11, 2014, from http://www.gamasutra.com/features/20010815/shelley_01.htm

Smith, K. (2014, April 3). Angry Birds Maker Rovio Reports $200 Million In Revenue, $71 Million In Profit for 2012. *Business Insider*, p. 1.

Soh, J. O., & Tan, B. C. (2008). Mobile Gaming. *Communications of the ACM, 51*(3), 35-39.

Tam, D. (2013, June 18). Candy Crush Saga creator appears sweet on an IPO. *CNET*, pp. 1-2.

Tassi, P. (2014, February 8). 'Flappy Bird' Creator says He's Taking The Game Down. *Forbes*, pp. 1-3.

Taylor-Powell, E., & Renner, M. (2003). Retrieved from Learning Store: http://learningstore.uwex.edu/assets/pdfs/g3658-12.pdf

Tellis, W. (1997). Application of a Case Study Methodology . *The Qualitative Report, 3*(3).

The Economist. (2013, April 27). Casual Games: Sweet Spot. *The Economist*. Retrieved 3 28, 2014, from http://www.economist.com/news/business/21576712-pretender-throne-world-casual-games-sweet-spot

Vincent, J. (2014, January 21). Candy Crush Saga creator King gets greedy and trademarks the word 'candy'. *The Independent*, pp. 1-2.

Winkler, T., & Buckner, K. (2006). Receptiveness of gamers to embedded brand messages in advergames: attitudes towards product placement. *Interactive Advertising, 7*(1), 24-32.

Wortham, J. (2010, December 11). Angry Birds, Flocking to Cellphones Everywhere. *The New York Times*, pp. 1-2.

Zucker, D. (2009). How to Do Case Study Research. *School of Nursing Faculty Publication Series, 2*.

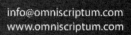

Printed by Books on Demand GmbH, Norderstedt / Germany